Become
an Inspirational Journal

Hope Mueller

Become

An Inspirational Journal

Copyright ©2021 by Hope Mueller

All rights reserved.

No part of this publication may be reproduced, stored in a retrieval system, or transmitted in any form or by any means—electronic, mechanical, photocopy, recording, or any other—without the prior permission of the author.

ISBN: 978-1-7372751-0-7

Printed in the United States of America

How to Become!

"This intersection is not your destination."
Barry Moze

This guided journal starts with goal setting, then write them down. We encourage and support you along the way. We take breaks to do fun, positive reinforcement activities. We reflect and focus on progress. We revise goals as needed and discuss our dreams. Then we celebrate!

Let's get started!

Goal Setting

(Excerpt from Counting Hope, From Conflict to Confidence)

"Let's get serious now." I instruct.

"Mom, really?"

"Yes, we are going to do this." I open the wooden book and flip to the next blank page. "We do this every year. I do not know why you are acting surprised."

Olivia groans but settles in, and Lauren curls into her lap. We include Lauren in goal setting although she is too young to fully participate.

"Got the coffee." Ashlei sets my cup down on the table and scoots in next to Olivia.

Brad is seated on the small couch, bouncing his leg, waiting to get started. "Come here, Brooke." He waves her over, she climbs up next to him and stops his leg from bouncing.

"Okay we will review our goals from last year then talk about this coming year." I begin. "Do we want to review the family goals first?"

"Sure. That is a good place to start."

Ashlei takes a sip of her coffee and listens.

We do this every year. We discuss our family, couple, and individual goals. It is common to do goal setting at work, less common for people to do goal setting with their families. My mom taught me goal setting early and I think it served as a key component to my success.

The first time we did goal setting as a family, everyone balked, now most of us look forward to the process. We are eager to review our accomplishments and enjoy the clarity that goal setting provides for the coming year.

Goal setting is not the answer to all life's complications and hardships. It is a process to define what you want your life to look like, to be. The process forces reflection, consciousness and prioritization.

The beauty is you do not have to wait for New Year's Eve to do it. You can pick it up anywhere, any day, any time. We have put together a 24-week guide to goal setting and focus, and to assist you in achieving your dreams. Here is to a fabulous 24- week journey filled with joy, success, and fulfillment.

Seven Steps to Goal Setting! Seven Steps to Becoming!

#1 Get Inspired!

What do you want your life to look like? What are your biggest dreams? What actions can you take these 24-weeks to move in the direction of those dreams and achievements? The best goals are a bit scary, challenging, but still motivating. Get excited about what you are going to accomplish in the coming weeks!

#2 Discuss and Decide

Chat through some ideas with your partner, mom, dad, siblings, colleagues, and friends. Whomever is on your *personal Board of Directors. These are the people who shape and impact your life. Importantly they are interested in seeing you succeed and be happy.

#3 Goal Setting

Traditional goal setting would tell you to set SMART goals: Specific, Measurable, Achievable, Relevant, and Timebound. These are good guidelines, however, my recommendation is a mix of straight forward SMART goals and a mix of dream goals. Setting both goal types ensure you have long-term dreams and immediate activities in sight. Go get 'em!

#4 WRITE IT DOWN

This is one of the most important steps. Write your goals down. This journal guides you. Studies show people are 40% more likely to achieve their goals if they are written down.

#5 Share

Talk about your goals. Post them on social media (if you want). Tell your partner, friends, family, colleagues, and your personal Board of Directors. Don't be shy. These folks love you. They want you to succeed and realize your dreams and goals!

---

* Personal Board of Directors is the group of people you routinely discuss your life, choices, and decisions with.

#6 Revisit and Reflect

Take a look periodically at your goals. This journal is designed for reflection periods, make sure to honor this time as much as the goal setting time. Discuss your progress with your personal Board of Directors. Adjust as necessary, these are YOUR goals. You can do what you want with them, change them, expand them, abandon them, and create new ones.

#7 Enjoy Your Success

Speaking from experience, this works. You move in the direction of your dreams. Your life takes the desired reality. You will be surprised and ecstatic with your progress in 24-weeks, or sooner!

Step #1:
Get Inspired!

If you had limitless money and limitless time, what would your life look like? What are your scariest goals? Biggest dreams? Most outlandish realities? The best goals are a bit scary, challenging, and still motivating. Get excited about what your life looks like and how it is going to get even better!

Describe your dream life- career, home and energy.

_____

_____

_____

_____

_____

_____

_____

_____

List 7 big ideas that seem almost impossible! *Some examples to get you started: Be a CEO of a 100M organization. Be a stay-at-home parent and take care of the kids full time.*

1. _____
2. _____
3. _____
4. _____
5. _____
6. _____
7. _____

Don't stop now! *Keep thinking through ideas, challenges, and exciting things that motivate you!*

_____
_____
_____
_____
_____
_____
_____
_____

Step #2:
Discuss & Decide

For goals to 'stick' you need to share them with people who know and love you. People who are invested in your success! These folks help solidify and clarify goals, and assist you in holding yourself accountable. Let's begin by naming your personal Board of Directors.

Board of Directors Title *Giving it a title forces you to name it and helps you talk about it with your board members. (example: Hopey's Board)*

_____

Next list your Board Members *Sometimes it is fun to include who they are, what you love about them, and how they support you. (example: Brad Mueller, Husband, Partner in this lifetime)*

_____

_____

_____

_____

_____

_____

_____

_____

_____

Don't stop now! Jot down how you might discuss your goals with the board members. Frequency, specificity, and what each member might help you with. (example: Bradley, review my company goals and budget, monthly)

_____

_____

_____

_____

_____

_____

_____

_____

_____

Step #3 and #4: Goal Setting and WRITE THEM DOWN!

Traditional goal setting would tell you to set SMART goals: Specific, Measurable, Achievable, Relevant, and Timebound. While these are good guidelines, we recommend a mix of straight forward SMART goals and a mix of dream goals. Setting these both keeps the emphasis on big dreams and tactical activities it takes to reach them. Go get 'em!

Three Dream Goals! *This gives voice and space for your dreams. (example: own a female leadership and development conference series/company)*

1. _____

_____

2. _____

_____

3. _____

_____

Five to Seven Tactical- Real Time Achievable-Goals! *Don't over do it, be clear, be concise, if this is your first time goal setting get finite and achievable. (example: one date night a month with Brad)*

_____

_____

_____

_____

_____

_____

_____

When? *Add due dates to each of the real time achievable goals.*

_____

_____

_____

_____

_____

_____

Don't stop now! *Refine your goals- how are you going to get your tactical goals completed?*

Step #5:
Share

Talk about your goals. Tell your personal Board of Directors, partners, friends, family, and colleagues. Don't be shy! These folks love you. They want to see you achieve your dreams!

Who/When? *Who will support you? Who are you going to share your dream goals with? When are you going to talk to them?*

_____

_____

_____

_____

_____

_____

_____

How? *How will you discuss it with them? Frequency?*

_____

_____

_____

_____

_____

_____

_____

_____

_____

Don't stop now! *Are you going to post them on Social Media? What else are you going to do to share and discuss your goals? Take a pic of your goals and post it #Become*

_____

_____

_____

_____

_____

_____

Step #6:
Revisit and Reflect

Post its? Other Reminders? *Where are you going to put reminders around in your life and environment? Post it reminders of big goals at your desk or bathroom- keep your goals front of mind!*

_____

_____

_____

_____

_____

_____

_____

_____

_____

_____

Step #7: Enjoy Your Success

This works! You move in the direction of your dreams. You will be surprised at what you achieve in 24-weeks.

You will succeed. Your life can and will look the way you want it. You are an incredible human, you can do fantastic things, no matter who you are. What you may have experienced or where you are at today, you can get this done, you can make this happen. You can make your dreams come true!

Something Fun!

List 10 (or 100) things YOU LOVE ABOUT YOURSELF!

_____
_____
_____
_____
_____
_____
_____
_____
_____
_____
_____
_____
_____
_____
_____
_____
_____
_____

Remember how awesome you are. You are astounding! No matter who you are, what you have experienced, or where you are at today—You got this! You can, and will, make your dreams come true.

Weekly Format

Intention

Each week we ask you to set a one-word intention for the week. This word shapes your purpose and objective for the week.

One Thing to Accomplish

If you only had one thing to accomplish this week what would it be? This helps you prioritize and focus your efforts and activities.

Personal Check In

This guides reflection on your well-being. This moment of reflection, and writing it down, hones emphasis and areas for adjustment.

Daily Prompts

Use this space for daily goals, intentions, areas to focus or celebration. Remember to celebrate your wins!

Reminders

Weekly reminders about your greatness and words of encouragement for you to relish.

Week 1: Let's Get Started!

Quote of the week:

"The secret of getting ahead is getting started."
Mark Twain

One word intention for the week: _____

One thing to accomplish this week: _____

_____

Personal check in: _____

_____

_____

_____

_____

Motivational Monday: _____

Transaction Tuesday: _____

Wild Wednesday:

Limitless Thursday: _____

Fantastic Friday: _____

Weekend Wrap Up or Other: _____

Reminders: We are just getting started. This is not a sprint but a marathon. Let's concentrate your mind, energy, and effort.

Week 2:
You got this!

Quote of the week:

"The strongest principle of growth lies in human choice."
George Eliot

One word intention for the week: _____

One thing to accomplish this week: _____

_____

Personal check in: _____

_____

_____

_____

_____

_____

Motivational Monday: _____

Transaction Tuesday: _____

Wild Wednesday:

Limitless Thursday: _____

Fantastic Friday: _____

Weekend Wrap Up or Other: _____

Reminders: Let's choose to grow this week. Who are you? Who do you want to be? What choices are you making this week to support your dreams?

Week 3: Become!

Quote of the week:

"I want to be all that I am capable of becoming."
Katherine Mansfield

One word intention for the week: _____

One thing to accomplish this week: _____

_____

Personal check in: _____

_____

_____

_____

_____

Motivational Monday: _____

Transaction Tuesday: _____

Wild Wednesday: _____

Limitless Thursday: _____

Fantastic Friday: _____

Weekend Wrap Up or Other: _____

Reminders: You are capable. You can do this! In fact you are doing this right now. You are becoming who you want to be each day.

Week 4: Light yourself on Fire!

Quote of the week:

"You must be ready to burn yourself in your own flame; how could you rise anew if you have not first become ashes?"
Friedrich Nietzsche

One word intention for the week: _____

One thing to accomplish this week: _____

_____

Personal check in: _____

_____

_____

_____

_____

_____

Motivational Monday: _____

Transaction Tuesday: _____

Wild Wednesday: _____

Limitless Thursday: _____

Fantastic Friday: _____

Weekend Wrap Up or Other: _____

Reminders: In order to transform you have to slough off the old and embrace the new. Purify yourself, get rid of bad habits and old negative ways of thinking. Burn brightly and move confidently into the future.

Check In! (Week 4)

Goal Progress. List the areas you have made progress on your goals. _____

_____

_____

_____

What areas did you want to make more progress in these first four weeks? _____

_____

_____

_____

There are no wrong answers. Be gentle, but persistent, with yourself. You will not realize all your dreams in four weeks. Are you making progress? Do you feel good?

Take the time to do a comprehensive personal check in. I use a ranking system for my 'check-ins'. Do what works for you 1-10 or A-F. Do whatever works to denote the current status of growth in each area.

Example of Hope's areas and rankings:

Exercise: 4

Water: 8

Diet (not weight loss, but healthy food choices and quantity): 5

Spiritual Practice: 1

Mom: 5

Wife: 6

Career: 9

Now that I type it, I can see it is super personal, and I am sharing this with you anyway. However, this practice works, first define the areas of your life to focus on. Just get started, these can change over time. Taking the time to do a personal check-in encourages honesty with yourself.

Week 5: *Be.*

Quote of the week:

"We are sharpened by our thoughts,
we become what we think."
Buddha

One word intention for the week: _____

One thing to accomplish this week: _____

_____

Personal check in: _____

_____

_____

_____

_____

Motivational Monday: _____

Transaction Tuesday: _____

Wild Wednesday: _____

Limitless Thursday:

Fantastic Friday: _____

Weekend Wrap Up or Other: _____

Reminders: Think good thoughts about yourself. You are what you think. You are what you concentrate on. Be focused on your good, your happiness, your strength, and your goals. "You become what you think." Buddha

Week 6: Positivity!

Quote of the week:

"Nothing can stop the man with the right mental attitude from achieving his goal; nothing on earth can help the man with the wrong mental attitude."
Thomas Jefferson

One word intention for the week: _____

One thing to accomplish this week: _____

_____

Personal check in: _____

_____

_____

_____

_____

Motivational Monday: _____

Transaction Tuesday: _____

Wild Wednesday:

Limitless Thursday: _____

Fantastic Friday: _____

Weekend Wrap Up or Other: _____

Reminders: There is no more powerful action than charging forward with a positive attitude. This builds belief in yourself and that goodness, joy and success is yours to have. Self-love is the foundation on which a joyful life is built upon. Be positive. Emphasize the good and more of it will come, it is already here.

Something Fun!

What 10 things have you improved on in the past 6 weeks? Or 10 things that are better than they were 6 weeks ago.

Can you believe it? Can you see how far you have come- already? Look at you go! Enjoy your achievement. Share it with your personal Board of Directors!

Week 7:
Your future

Quote of the week:

"The best way to predict the future is to create it."
Abraham Lincoln

One word intention for the week: _____

One thing to accomplish this week: _____

_____

Personal check in: _____

_____

_____

_____

_____

_____

Motivational Monday: _____

Transaction Tuesday: _____

Wild Wednesday: _____

Limitless Thursday: _____

Fantastic Friday: _____

Weekend Wrap Up or Other: _____

Reminders: You have the gift of being able to create your future. You can build the life you want to build. In fact- YOU ALREADY ARE! Right now today, the past few weeks (and probably a lifetime before) you are constructing your future. You are doing it. Reflect and appreciate on how fabulous you are and what you are creating.

Week 8:
Live. Really Live!

Quote of the week:

> "There is always a risk in being alive,
> and if you are more alive, there is more risk."
> **Henrik Ibsen**

One word intention for the week: _____

One thing to accomplish this week: _____

_____

Personal check in: _____

_____

_____

_____

_____

Motivational Monday: _____

Transaction Tuesday: _____

Wild Wednesday: _____

Limitless Thursday: _____

Fantastic Friday: _____

Weekend Wrap Up or Other: _____

Reminders: As you grow the more joy you gain. Be alive. Hiding or avoiding risk, is safe, but does not increase your happiness or the joy you share with those around you. Be bold. Be willing to live life fully and expand your joy.

Week 9:
Love is for you.

Quote of the week:

"You yourself as much as anybody in the entire universe deserve your love and affection"
Buddha

One word intention for the week: _____

One thing to accomplish this week: _____

_____

Personal check in: _____

_____

_____

_____

_____

Motivational Monday: _____

Transaction Tuesday: _____

Wild Wednesday: _____

Limitless Thursday: _____

Fantastic Friday: _____

Weekend Wrap Up or Other: _____

Reminders: You deserve joy. You deserve victory. You are worthy of all the good the world has to offer. Take it, revel in it, and enjoy it.

Week 10:
The amazing you!

Quote of the week:

"Be yourself; everyone else is already taken."
Oscar Wilde

One word intention for the week: _____

One thing to accomplish this week: _____

_____

Personal check in: _____

_____

_____

_____

_____

_____

_____

Motivational Monday: _____

Transaction Tuesday: _____

Wild Wednesday:

Limitless Thursday: _____

Fantastic Friday: _____

Weekend Wrap Up or Other: _____

_____
_____
_____
_____
_____
_____
_____
_____
_____
_____
_____
_____

Reminders: This quote is so obvious. What we miss is the fact that you are amazing, you are awesome, and perfect exactly as you are. You are beautiful, strong, and full of light. Be your miraculous light filled self. Love yourself unabashedly it allows people to love themselves around you.

Something Fun!

If you could do anything tomorrow what would it be? Why?

_____
_____
_____
_____
_____
_____
_____
_____
_____
_____
_____
_____
_____
_____
_____
_____
_____
_____

How does this something fun build into your goals? Is it part of it? Does your dreams and goals align with this thing you want to do tomorrow? Why can't you do it tomorrow? If you can, you should. DO THE THING! If you cant, what can you do similar to it? If you are not doing it tomorrow, go write it in on a date on your calendar and plan for it, and make it happen.

Week 11:
All the way!

Quote of the week:

"There are only two mistakes one can make along the road to truth: not going all the way, and not starting."
Buddha

One word intention for the week: _____

One thing to accomplish this week: _____

_____

Personal check in: _____

_____
_____
_____
_____

Motivational Monday: _____

Transaction Tuesday: _____

Wild Wednesday: _____

Limitless Thursday:

Fantastic Friday: _____

Weekend Wrap Up or Other: _____

Reminders: You have gotten started. Now push through and keep going. All the way. Long past the duration of this journal (you could always buy a second one!). Go all the way. Persevere through the valleys and know the hilltop is there for you to climb if you keep taking the steps forward.

Week 12: Live Fully!

Quote of the week:

"To live is so startling it leaves little time for anything else."
Emily Dickinson

One word intention for the week: _____

One thing to accomplish this week: _____

_____

Personal check in: _____

_____

_____

_____

_____

_____

Motivational Monday: _____

Transaction Tuesday: _____

Wild Wednesday: _____

Limitless Thursday: _____

Fantastic Friday: _____

Weekend Wrap Up or Other: _____

Reminders: Wow! Look at you living, being fully yourself, and making such progress. I love it! So proud and excited for you.

Check In! (Twelve weeks)

Go back to pages 13-16 and transcribe the goals you listed there

_____

_____

_____

_____

_____

_____

_____

_____

_____

_____

Be gentle and persistent. You will not accomplish all of your goals in one quarter. The question is you making progress and do you feel good?

Where have you made progress on your dreams?

_____

_____

_____

_____

What areas were you hoping for more?

_____

_____

_____

_____

Deep dive personal check in. List the areas of your life and do a quick ranking of how you think you are doing.

_____

_____

_____

_____

_____

_____

_____

_____

_____

_____

_____

_____

Now lets check. Do these goals still work for you? Is there something you want to abandon or something to add? Unlikely you want to throw them all out and start over, but maybe there is one or two goals that either need to be let go or tweaked to better define your direction.

_____
_____
_____
_____
_____
_____
_____
_____
_____
_____
_____
_____
_____
_____
_____
_____
_____

Week 13:
Storms shmorms. Psshh.

Quote of the week:

> "I am not afraid of storms for
> I am learning how to sail my ship."
> **Louisa May Alcott**

One word intention for the week: _____

One thing to accomplish this week: _____

_____

Personal check in: _____

_____

_____

_____

_____

_____

Motivational Monday: _____

Transaction Tuesday: _____

Wild Wednesday: _____

Limitless Thursday: _____

Fantastic Friday: _____

Weekend Wrap Up or Other: _____

Reminders: There are bumps in the road. You will hit storms. Let them come. Know that regardless of what is coming, know you will persevere. You will succeed. The winds may blow but you are ready when the winds die down. You are destined to find your joy and triumph.

Week 14: Why am I so mean to myself?

Quote of the week:

*"Our greatest enemies,
the ones we must fight most often, are within."*
Thomas Paine

One word intention for the week: _____

One thing to accomplish this week: _____

_____

Personal check in: _____

_____
_____
_____
_____

Motivational Monday: _____

Transaction Tuesday: _____

Wild Wednesday: _____

Limitless Thursday: _____

Fantastic Friday: _____

Weekend Wrap Up or Other: _____

_____

_____

_____

_____

_____

_____

_____

_____

_____

_____

_____

_____

_____

_____

Reminders: Why are so hard on ourselves? Why don't we know we are beautiful and powerful? Why do we have to work so hard to accept our greatness? The truth is there. Find ways to move past your insecurities and fears. Deploy habits to remind you to appreciate yourself. If it is writing positive phrases about yourself everyday do that. Be conscience of when you are unnecessarily hard on yourself, then stop it and know better. Enjoy being you. Because you are fabulous!

Week 15: Want It!

Quote of the week:

"I want to do it because I want to do it."
Amelia Earhart

One word intention for the week: _____

One thing to accomplish this week: _____

_____

Personal check in: _____

_____

_____

_____

_____

_____

_____

Motivational Monday: _____

Transaction Tuesday: _____

Wild Wednesday: _____

Limitless Thursday: _____

Fantastic Friday: _____

Weekend Wrap Up or Other: _____

Reminders: Sometimes we are afraid to say what we want. Be encouraged to say what you want. Tell your Board of Directors, tell you friends and family, and certainly tell yourself. It is ok to want something big and bold astounding. You want it, go get it.

Week 16: Work!

Quote of the week:

"Success is not something to wait for,
it is something to work for."
Henry Wadsworth Longfellow

One word intention for the week: _____

One thing to accomplish this week: _____

_____

Personal check in: _____

_____

_____

_____

_____

Motivational Monday: _____

Transaction Tuesday: _____

Wild Wednesday: _____

Limitless Thursday: _____

Fantastic Friday: _____

Weekend Wrap Up or Other:

Reminders: Obvious statement but you must work for success. Be willing to do the work, start the work, and keep at it. It is there for you. All the joy and success you want, is there for you, go get it!

Something Fun!

Name 10 (or 100) things you love about your career!

_____
_____
_____
_____
_____
_____
_____
_____
_____
_____
_____
_____
_____
_____
_____
_____
_____
_____
_____
_____

Success in your career builds on itself. The more you do well, the more you do, and the success piles on. This establishes your passions by building a positive feedback loop.

Week 17:
Know. Be. Do.

Quote of the week:

"Knowing is not enough; we must apply,
Willing is not enough; we must do."
Johann Wolfgang von Goethe

One word intention for the week: _____

One thing to accomplish this week: _____

_____

Personal check in: _____

_____

_____

_____

_____

Motivational Monday: _____

Transaction Tuesday: _____

Wild Wednesday: _____

Limitless Thursday: _____

Fantastic Friday: _____

Weekend Wrap Up or Other: _____

Reminders: Thinking, hoping, dreaming is great but it must turn into action. Actions make progress. You must do the things you WANT to do. Move forward, make progress, do it.

Week 18: Dream on!

Quote of the week:

> "We all have our own life to pursue,
> our own kind of dream to be weaving."
> Loiusa May Alcott

One word intention for the week: _____

One thing to accomplish this week: _____

_____

Personal check in: _____

_____

_____

_____

_____

Motivational Monday: _____

Transaction Tuesday: _____

Wild Wednesday: _____

Limitless Thursday: _____

Fantastic Friday: _____

Weekend Wrap Up or Other: _____

Reminders: Your dreams are achievable. Right now today, this week, the past few weeks you have been taking real steps to realize your dreams. You got this! You are doing it right now.

Something Fun!

What 10 (or 100) things do you love about your body?

You are beautiful. Know this. Believe it. Relish it. No one is you. You are exactly as you were meant to be. Savor your beauty.

Glance Forward

We have stopped and reflected on our progress a few times. Now let's lift our heads and look forward. How much further will we go and how are our lives and goals evolving?

One year from now I will:

_____
_____
_____
_____
_____
_____
_____
_____
_____

Five years from now I will:

_____
_____
_____
_____

_____

_____

_____

_____

_____

_____

When I am in the final stages of my life what do I want to look back and see? (Legacy statement)

_____

_____

_____

_____

_____

_____

_____

_____

Close your eyes. Envision your life the way you want it. Use as much detail and description as you can to fully flesh out your dream life. Don't wait for the next writing prompt, spend time doing this every week. Talk about this vision with the closest members of your personal Board of Directors. Own this reality.

Week 19: Garden of joy!

Quote of the week:

"Don't judge each day by the harvest
you reap but by the seeds that you plant."
Robert Louis Stevenson

One word intention for the week: _____

One thing to accomplish this week: _____

_____

Personal check in: _____

_____

_____

_____

_____

_____

Motivational Monday: _____

_____
_____
_____
_____
_____
_____
_____
_____
_____
_____
_____
_____
_____
_____
_____
_____
_____
_____
_____

Transaction Tuesday: _____

Wild Wednesday: _____

Limitless Thursday: _____

Fantastic Friday:

Weekend Wrap Up or Other: _____

_____

_____

_____

_____

_____

_____

_____

_____

_____

_____

_____

_____

_____

_____

_____

_____

_____

_____

Reminders: You are planting seeds for your joy and success. Everyday. They will grow and you get to enjoy the fruits of your labor. And don't forget to relish the gardening and labor of love. You will look back and think "Wow! I did that!" I got that done! Look what I made happen.

Week 20:
This is an exciting week. Why? Because you get to live it! Experience this week.

Quote of the week:

"When you arise in the morning, think of what a precious privilege it is to be alive- to breathe, to think, to enjoy, to love."

Marcus Aurelius

One word intention for the week: _____

One thing to accomplish this week: _____

_____

Personal check in: _____

_____

_____

Motivational Monday: _____

Transaction Tuesday: _____

Wild Wednesday: _____

Limitless Thursday: _____

Fantastic Friday: _____

Weekend Wrap Up or Other: _____

Reminders: You are here. You are living fully. You are loving, progressing, and stretching your life. You are so impressive!

Week 21: Create the warmth you want to feel!

Quote of the week:

"If the world seems cold to you, kindle fires to warm it."
Lucy Larcom

One word intention for the week: _____

One thing to accomplish this week: _____

_____

Personal check in: _____

_____

_____

_____

_____

_____

Motivational Monday: _____

Transaction Tuesday: _____

Wild Wednesday: _____

Limitless Thursday: _____

Fantastic Friday: _____

Weekend Wrap Up or Other: _____

Reminders: Each of us has the power to bring joy or pain to those around us. Chose wisely. Joy building creates more happiness and more triumphs. Be the reason someone smiles or has a great day or week.

Week 22: Keep Believing!

Quote of the week:

> "We all have the power to make wishes come true, as long as we keep believing."
> **Louisa May Alcott**

One word intention for the week: _____

One thing to accomplish this week: _____

_____

Personal check in: _____

_____

_____

_____

_____

_____

Motivational Monday: _____

Transaction Tuesday: _____

Wild Wednesday:

Limitless Thursday: _____

Fantastic Friday:

Weekend Wrap Up or Other: _____

Reminders: Journey was right, their song has the right words and the music swells your emotions. Take a drive this week, play the song full blast, with all of the windows open! Don't stop believing!

Something Fun!

What 10 (or 100) things do you love about your life?

The importance of paying attention to the good cannot be understated. This is your life. Your life to live, to enjoy and to be fulfilled. Love your life. Remind yourself of all of the good things you have and are thankful for.

Week 23: Take it!

Quote of the week:

"Seize the moments of happiness, love and be loved! That is the only reality in the world, all else is folly."
Leo Tolstoy

One word intention for the week: _____

One thing to accomplish this week: _____

_____

Personal check in: _____

_____
_____
_____
_____
_____

Motivational Monday: _____

Transaction Tuesday: _____

Wild Wednesday: _____

Limitless Thursday: _____

Fantastic Friday: _____

Weekend Wrap Up or Other: _____

Reminders: Happiness is yours to have, yours to take. Don't wait for happiness to fall from the sky. Give yourself the gift of enjoying moments, relishing joy, and happiness and wresting it to your breast. Hold tight because it is yours.

Week 24:
Born for this.

Quote of the week:

> "I am not afraid; I was born to do this."
> **Joan of Arc**

One word intention for the week: _____

One thing to accomplish this week: _____

_____

Personal check in: _____

_____

_____

_____

_____

_____

Motivational Monday:

Transaction Tuesday: _____

Wild Wednesday: _____

Limitless Thursday: _____

Fantastic Friday: _____

Weekend Wrap Up or Other: _____

Reminders: You were born for joy and love. You were born for happiness. Push past your fears and live courageously. Let the success come to you.

Check In! (Twenty four weeks)

Go back to pages 13 - 16 and transcribe the goals

_____
_____
_____
_____
_____
_____
_____
_____

Be persistent. You will not attain all of your goals in two quarters. Are you making progress? Do you feel good?

Where have you made progress on your dreams?

_____
_____
_____
_____

What areas were you hoping for more progress?

_____

_____

_____

_____

Deep dive personal check in. List the areas of your life and rank of how you think you are doing in each area.

_____

_____

_____

_____

_____

_____

_____

_____

_____

_____

You have concentrated on these goals for 24 weeks! What an accomplishment. You are encouraged to keep going. Establish year long goals, or do another 24 week set, do whatever works for you, but keep going. Do not lose the momentum and victories you have gained thus far. You got this!

Finale!

Final quote:

"I've been a woman for a little over 50 years and have gotten over my initial astonishment."
Nadia Boulanger

Twenty-four? Why end at twenty-four? I don't know about you, but I find writing in one journal for a whole year to be a real feat! Even 24 weeks can be a stretch. Once habits are established, then they can be maintained. I am guessing there were pieces of this that worked great for you and others not-so-much. You can buy a cheap pad of paper and keep up the practices that work for you. Or buy a beautiful, lined journal, with no prompts, and do the same. If you wish, if it works for you, you loved it, you can buy another journal to cover the next 24 weeks.

My friends, I am wildly hopeful in the joy, success, reassurance and support you have found in these pages, in these activities, and over these weeks together.

No matter who you are. No matter where you are. No matter what you have experienced. You are marvelous. You are powerful. Your life is happiness and more can be found. Know it. Embrace it. Be it. Become.

About the Author:

Hope Mueller is an author, inspirational speaker, executive, and active non-for-profit volunteer. Hope leads a pharmaceutical consulting firm and is the founder of Hunter Street Charity. She lives with her husband in Northern Illinois and enjoys parenting her four daughters and grandson. 10% of gross sales for Hopey, Counting Hope, and Become are donated to Hunter Street Charity.

Please connect with Hope:

Facebook: Hope Mueller, Author

Twitter: @hpmueller242

Instagram: @hpmueller242

GoodReads: Hope Mueller

Linked In: Hope Mueller, H2M LLC, and Hunter Street Charity

Websites: www.hopey.net, www.hunterstreetcharity.com

Email: hope@hopey.net, tiffany@hopey.net

www.ingramcontent.com/pod-product-compliance
Lightning Source LLC
Chambersburg PA
CBHW072148100526
44589CB00015B/2132